Genre Story

Essential Question
What choices are good for us?

The Gift of Weaving
A Navajo Story

retold by Lana Jones • illustrated by Lisa Desimini

Chapter 1
Searching for Help 2

Chapter 2
Learning to Weave 7

Chapter 3
Finding the Answer .12

Respond to Reading 16

PAIRED READ How to Weave Paper Mats 17

Focus on Genre 20

Chapter 1
Searching for Help

Once, the Navajo people didn't know how to weave. Sometimes it was too cold to collect plants or hunt animals. Navajo families were cold and hungry all winter.

Two women wanted to save their families. They decided to ask the **wise** ones for help. But the wise ones lived far away.

The women set off on their journey.

After walking for many days, they got lost. "Help!" they called out hopelessly. "Someone help us!"

STOP AND CHECK

Why did the women go on a journey?

Suddenly, a woman **appeared** on a cliff above them. She wove a strong rope. She threw the rope down over the women. Then she pulled them up to the top.

"I am Spider Woman. How are you?" she asked them.

"Our families have no food," said one of the women. "Can you help us?"

"I will help," said Spider Woman. "But you must do what I say."

Spider Woman asked the women to bring four thick branches. The bottom branch became Earth. The top branch became the Sky. The side branches held up the sky. She wound a **graceful** web up and down. This brought Earth and Sky together.

Spider Woman also made tools for the women to use for weaving.

"You can use this loom to weave," she said.

STOP AND CHECK

How did Spider Woman make the loom?

Chapter 2
Learning to Weave

The women were confused.

"How will a loom feed our people?" they asked.

"Watch what I do," said Spider Woman.

Spider Woman wove another rope. She threw it over some sheep. She showed the women how to take the wool off the sheep. Then she explained how to make the wool into yarn.

One of the women **interrupted** her. "Our people can't eat yarn," she said.

"Sometimes help comes in a way you do not **expect**," Spider Woman said.

She helped the women make dyes from leaves and berries. She told them how to dye the yarn. Finally, she taught them how to use the loom to weave a blanket.

"Do the best you can. Don't be careless and make mistakes," Spider Woman said.

The women loved weaving. They became fast weavers. They worked for days. They did not notice time passing. They forgot their families.

Then Spider Woman said, "You cannot only weave in life. From now on, make one mistake in your weaving. That way, you will not forget other things."

STOP AND CHECK

Why must the women make a mistake?

Chapter 3
Finding the Answer

"Now we can make blankets," one of the women said.

"How will blankets feed our people?" asked the other one.

"Go home. Then you will understand," Spider Woman said.

So they went home and taught their families how to weave. They showed them all the things that Spider Woman had shown them.

> **STOP AND CHECK**
>
> What did the two women teach their families?

The people wove blankets for their families and friends. They created beautiful **patterns**. The blankets kept them warm. The people made more blankets than they needed. They traded extra blankets for food and other goods. They became healthy and happy. At last, the two women figured out how Spider Woman had helped them.

The women cooked a **flavorful** meal to thank Spider Woman. They took the food to the place Spider Woman lived. The **luscious aroma drifted** around the cliffs.

They knew Spider Woman was there, though they could not see her. They gave her thanks for all she had done. They left the food for her.

For the rest of their lives, they thanked Spider Woman for the gift of weaving.

> **STOP AND CHECK**
>
> How did the two women thank Spider Woman?

Respond to Reading

Summarize

Summarize the main events of this story. Use your chart if you wish.

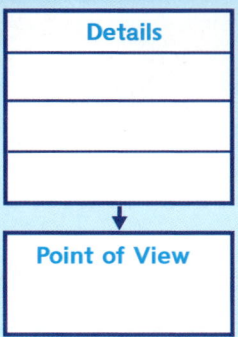

Text Evidence

1. Reread page 14. How do you think the women feel about Spider Woman's gift now? POINT OF VIEW

2. Find the word *careless* on page 8. What does it mean? What clues help you figure it out? ROOT WORDS

3. Write about what happened when the women asked for help. Did they get the help they expected? WRITE ABOUT READING

Genre Directions

Compare Texts
Read about making paper mats.

How to Weave Paper Mats

The skill of weaving has been around for a long time. People weave baskets and rugs. You can weave a paper dinner mat.

What You Need:

- Two pieces of colored paper. Each piece should be 12 inches long and 9 inches wide.
- Ruler
- Pencil
- Scissors

What to Do:

1. Fold one sheet of paper in half.

2. Draw a line that is 1 inch from the edge.

3. Make even-spaced cuts up to the line.

4. Take the second sheet of paper. Cut strips that are 9 inches long and 1 inch wide.

5. Unfold the first sheet of paper. Weave a strip over and under the cuts in the first sheet of paper.

6. Weave the next strip through the paper. Switch the order when you go over and under.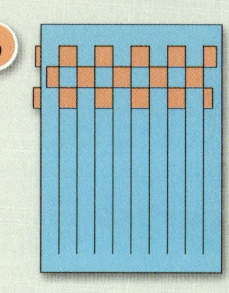

7. Keep weaving the strips. Be sure to switch the order each time.

Use a **variety** of colors for your mats. Enjoy the **healthful** food you can eat on them!

Make Connections

How has weaving helped people in the past? ESSENTIAL QUESTION

The women in the story wove blankets. You wove dinner mats. What other things can people weave? TEXT TO TEXT

Focus on Genre

Stories Traditional stories help people pass their customs, beliefs, and teachings to others. These stories teach children how to live and think. They may have events that seem unusual.

Read and Find *The Gift of Weaving* is a story with a character who can do magical things. In real life, the Navajo people are very skilled weavers.

Your Turn

What lesson does this story teach? Why is it important?